F Bombs 4 Single Moms

F-ing your way to happy

Christina Ciani

IamthatIam Publishing

F Bombs 4 Single Moms

The FiZGiGs and author appreciate your support!

ISBN-13: 978-0-9794930-2-7

ISBN-10: 0-9794930-2-1

Library of Congress Control Number:
2011903389

Mail letters, insights or questions to:
Iamthatlam Publishing
PO Box 20811
Columbus, OH 43220

Or visit:

www.IamthatlamPublishing.com

www.FbombMoms.com

For S. and E.
Who reminded me of the Truths of Youth.
You make life a joy and change my world with your insights...
Never stop living your dreams - I love you -

and for all the women F Bombing to change their world for the better:
you can do this.

Who cares?

Acknowledgments

People care. I promise. Some of the people who show up for me...

YOU

You and your child matter to me. I don't want you to think you're alone in this, because you're not. We're in this together. There are millions of women who want you to succeed, and I'm one of them. Don't give up - I believe in you.

my parents

Pat and Sam

They taught me the meaning of unconditional love. Though they've had their hands full at times, they keep their chins up and their hearts open through everything. I learned from their example: anything is possible.

my brother

Tim

Tim is living proof that angels still exist. I can't think of any other reason someone would walk away from their life (in sunny Florida) and move to Ohio to help me and my sons. He showed up, stuck it out with us and continues to be a positive force in our lives. I am blessed to be his sister.

my friends, including

Michelle, Anna, Cathey, Alicia, Jayn & Alana

I think the best things in life are invisible. Trust. Friendship. Love. Laughter. Hope. Kindness. Reliability. Joy. Our friendship keeps me going. Thank you for believing in me, and caring about my family, even when you had your hands full, too.

The Seeker

A dear friend and advisor. If it wasn't for his insights, humor, teachings and kindness I wouldn't understand the value of Peace.

editor, consultant and more

Becky Blanton

Becky is the down to earth voice that says, "Keep going, you can do this!!!" Her story from homelessness to an ever growing career as a writer, TED Global 2009 Speaker, editor, designer and consultant will inspire you and change you forever. Thank you for everything, Becky.

creative assistance

Ian Stewart

Ian donated his time to offer insight and creative ideas that helped focus my work, vision and writing. His help has been priceless. I keep my notes from our talk by my desk as a constant reminder to stay focused and upbeat.

pay it forward

Rabbi Issamar Ginzberg

Rabbi Ginzberg asked some people to Pay it Forward in 2011. This great idea inspired Ian to share his wisdom with me, and I am forever grateful for this priceless gift.

ideaschema design genius

Megan Elizabeth Morris

Design is her work, but her passion for art you can connect with makes the difference. Some people layout a book, but Megan has crafted an experience you can enjoy and cherish. She didn't just put it together, she put her heart into it. This book wouldn't have reached you without her and Ideaschema.com.

the man who

Seth Godin

Seth inspires millions of people to do the work that it takes to make a positive difference. His books, blog and innovative ideas have changed the world - for the better. I have learned more in one year from him than I learned in college... and I've never met him.

Thanks, Seth. I shipped.

Thank you Triiibes.

Contents

"Shit fuck damn"

There, we've said them.

The next time you need them they'll be available.
But what next? What do you think, say or do AFTER "shit fuck damn"?

Forget what you've heard, you're NOT a single mom.
You are a woman raising a child, learning what that means, figuring out how to do it right and how to make magic out of pure shit. That's amazing. You are making the world a better place and you're not a label, a loser or a lost cause. You with me?

YOU ARE YOU and you're allowed to be happy.

F Bombs are a way to change our minds. What we know, what we've learned in the past, isn't necessarily going to help us become remarkable achievers or daily divas of magical living. This list of 27 words and their use, are going to help you, if you use them every day, to be happier and better at everything you do. Reprogramming what we think changes problems into possibilities.

WAIT! Before you run or roll your eyes answer this question:

Are you happy? Right here, right now? If you don't feel happiness where you are, I understand.

I have been swimming in dirty diapers, buried under bills, had screaming men in my face, dealt with uncaring day cares and an empty refrigerator. I've also wondered, "How the hell can a monk sit on a mountain and be happy or a child sit in a pile of mud laughing, but I can't seem to find Bliss anywhere in my life?"

F Bombs will help you do it.

Since you're going to be thinking something today - isn't it about time you tried something that might help?

F your misery and change your mind.

Passion 4 changing your words

WHY change your words?

F Bombs are words you use to keep your thoughts busy on things that are important for freedom and happiness. Internal or external, having any kind of freedom requires we acknowledge it's okay to be free, and that freedom for our kids means freedom for ourselves first. Being happy means we work to get rid of the negatives standing in our way. I can't be happy and full of sorrow at the same time. Everything we need to do, that we must do, to experience our lives as exciting, worth getting up for and worth engaging in with everything we've got, is FREE. It's our perspective as single mothers that changes our experience. Once we realize this, and work on it, a huge weight drops off our shoulders.

I'm NOT a single mom!

I don't like the terms "single mom," "lone mother," "sole parent," or "divorcee."

They imply there might be something missing in our lives - like we're half real. They are jaded, outdated and demeaning. I'm throwing them away and replacing them with terms like "warrior woman," "ARt teacher," "soul shaper," "world changer," "MamaGood," "3D guardian angel" and FiZGiG - my favorite.

FiZGiG replaces motherhood (that archaic 'woe is me' past) from something that was seen as almost disgusting when you do it alone, to a life of upbeat nurturing what the entire world is after: a good life. Leave motherhood for the traditional married masses. I'm on the road of FiZGiGing with all my sisters and creating a better world by changing how we live our lives - one thought at a time.

WHO are we?

RU a single mom, mum, mother, lone parent, or welfare wench living with poverty or in a world of hatred?

Are you suffering, every day through massive chores, job restrictions, day care hells and disconnections from your children? Are you drifting through life in a hurried rush, trying to sleep, eat, clean, and find help while simultaneously cursing people who don't know what to say or how to help you?

Are you tired of people who don't understand that all you want to do is try to find a small break so you can have just 10 minutes of uninterrupted happiness with your child before the sun goes down?

If you're struggling with all of this, like I do every day, then maybe it's time we start helping one another. Freedom doesn't come easily, but it does come if you work at it. We can do many things on our own, or with each other's help, that might seem impossible. We've been duped into believing the idea is to amass wealth, accumulate property, trinkets and status symbols that give us a false sense of worth. There is a trick to all of this. Self worth can't be bought. No matter who we are, where we've been living or what we've already (barely) gotten through - it's time we had a taste of the best in life - without spending every penny we have or wasting one more thought on what we don't know about tomorrow.

I've been raising my two sons on my own for 10 years. I don't have a lot of patience for convention, and I am not one to pretend you can make heaven out of hell all in one day. I've learned a few, simple and masterful tricks for avoiding stress, frustration and worry. I'm sharing them with you here, because they can help you transform your life into an adventure that deserves to be lived. I wish I'd known then what I know now.

I'm asking two things of you:

Read through it - even if you feel frantic, panicky or pressed to move on to your next stressful meeting, task, or go looking for a new way to feel good. Unless it involves attending to your child, I'm asking you to give this at least a quick once over. You won't be missing out on much out there in your world, and you can spare the time needed to read through this.

Believe in yourself. I believe in you. This is what no one gave me in the beginning. No one wanted me to succeed on my terms, to run my life as I saw fit. I was only told how I failed, how I wasn't measuring up to standards I knew nothing about, and how I wasn't even coming close to what "other people" told me I should be doing. Single motherhood is a painful enough way to grow up FAST, especially when you're doing your best to raise a child so they learn to thrive. It's even harder to do if you have to deal with the onslaught of challenges and attacks that come with poverty, isolation or fear in what I call the "invisible prison." Most women and girls cannot move from their town or state. It's "make it or break it" where you already live. It takes some effort, but I know you can find the way to make your life work - cheaply, wonderfully and joyfully. I know it because I do it - every F-ing day of my life. I want you to feel as great as I do. Your child deserves happy memories, but equally important - so do you. I believe in you, even if you don't believe me - yet.

We need to feel good whether we are shoveling shit, wiping butts or dealing with welfare. We need to feel that we matter, to know that we count, and that we have something to say. We need to be willing to work (yes, sorry, there is some thinking work to do - but that is all there is - no push ups or time consuming check lists - just thoughts. That's all you have to do with me here).

WHAT WAS I THINKING?!

I can wash dishes or clothes and be talking to myself about how this thought or the next one is negative.

Then, I have to realize I can choose what thoughts I want to give my time to and what thoughts I want, or don't want, to express. When your ex is screaming in your face you simply say, in your mind, "Hmmm...what an ass he's being, and right to my face again. Isn't this interesting." You don't say anything out loud. You don't engage in the conversation! You decide you have a right to choose your words.

Sometimes, whether you hear the whole comment from your ex, your mother or anyone else who is being ridiculous with you or not, it's painful to listen to them and believe in the power of F Bombs, but believe it. You do have the power to change your thoughts and your words, which will change your life. I know it. I do it all the time.

F Bombs are words you use to keep your thoughts busy on things that are important for freedom and happiness. Freedom and happiness come from within. You don't buy them, you become them. To feel free in our lives we need to give ourselves permission to be free in our minds FIRST. To be happy we have to get rid of all the negative tapes we are playing in our heads. They're in our way. We can't think two thoughts at once - I can't be happy and full of sorrow at the same time. We can, and we have to, choose.

Since I've been using these words to change my mind, I've noticed unpleasant events still occur - but I'm not imprisoned by them. I don't spend three days worrying about how I'll deal with the next rent payment or how I'll pay the day care or confront an issue that frightens me. Instead, I've found I can see every obstacle as an opportunity to grow into the person I want to be - the woman I want to remember and the woman, mother and person my children deserve to know.

An important part of reaching your dreams is giving them your attention, giving them your time, giving them the ability to crack open, sprout, flower and bear the sweet, unique fruit that is you.

If we spend our lives complaining, moaning, bitching, wishing and praying for some magical wand to appear and turn it into a wonderland, we're forgetting that we are that magical wand.

We are the magical wand that turns frowns into smiles. We are the magical wand that turns cries into comfort.

We're it!

FUN DA MENTALS

THE BASICS

Keep your fundamental, happiness-stimulating tools easily accessible. These are the things you will need to keep foremost in your mind, so you don't forget them. This is the most important thing you can do to keep the vision of a happier you where you need to see it during tough times. It's too easy to get off track or distracted by "the next great idea." Your goals, friends, job, home and appearance will probably change, but your fundamental good feelings, your "I want to experience this in my life" realities, deserve to be constantly remembered. People who know what lifts them up and makes them feel good, what makes their health vibrant, what music soothes their soul or lifts their mood always have a supply of fundamental stimulants. They keep them on hand always - just in case.

KEEP THE DUH (DA) OUT

Don't be a fool. Drugs. Alcohol. Fake fingernails. Prestige. Fame. Fortune. These are things you can live without and still be at your best. The things you can't live without: Peace. The ability to calm yourself. A song that always lifts your spirits. A story, memory or photo that reminds you: life is good. Fundamentals are non-negotiable truths for you. If you are a spiritual person a prayer, hymn, mantra, affirmation or a creed might instantly bring your attention back to basic goodness - no matter what mess is surrounding you today.

FUNDAMENTALS: MENTAL FUN

FUNDAMENTALS: FUN MENTAL STIMULANTS THAT TRAVEL WITH YOU.

If you don't have a way to remember them easily, you might forget you have them at all. I surround our home with images, stones, music and books so, on any given day, I won't find myself weaponless against fear or frustration. If you don't have a working array of fundamental, happiness-stimulating tools, get them out in front of you.

SOME FUN-DA-MENTAL IDEAS

Quotes on your refrigerator & bathroom mirror
A necklace or ring as a reminder
(I have a ring that has Happiness written on the inside)
CDs or songs that ALWAYS make you feel better
Invisible & free thoughts to remember:
No matter how bad it gets, I'm going to make my life great
I know God is laughing, just waiting to see what miracle I pull off next
What would Buddha do?
Mother Theresa had problems, too
Whatever I do, I'm not going to let them see me sweat
"Great! Now I get to see what a genius I really am!"
"This ought to get interesting...and fast."
OK, if I was a Superhero...what would I do next?
Refuse ornate & expensive until you master simple appreciation
Find bliss in something ordinary
Don't go without (outside yourself) for entertainment
A lot of "things" does not equal a lot of Happiness
Madonna wouldn't put up with this shit
Ellen would love to see this on her show

Whatever moves us toward solutions has a chance of working.

"A chance?!" you might say. . . well . . . it's up to you to keep moving and not get stuck, even if the next roadblock looks bigger. If it IS bigger it might be because you can actually handle it – time to find out, isn't it?

FAMILY

IT'S SECOND

Family is second because if you aren't fundamentally stable, happy, focused and healthy nothing works well.

We spend our time trying to change and alter our outside reality and ignore the inner stuff too much. We battle invisible dragons (depression, addiction, people's moods and fear) but don't take the time to get our minds to a place where we can create positive change. This is a masterful way to create a family experience that works - for everyone we love.

Get right inside of you, and then expand that right, good feeling to others in your family circle FIRST. The world might ask you to show up and offer your best on any given day (and it does) but we have to show up for ourselves and our children FIRST.

WHY FAMILY

If you have to ask, then you deserve an answer.

I'd like to assume we all get it already, but in my experience most women doing the FiZGiG dance on their own have no idea how important these baby steps are. We work on ourselves, work on relating and building relationships that matter and thrive with our child, then we put whatever energy is left over out into the marketplace called "the rest of the world." If that doesn't make sense to you, it's okay. It doesn't make sense to most people - yet. Here's the deal: we all want a good experience of life, right? We all want to be happy, too. With only 24 hours in a day - choose your playing field wisely. Every move you make toward feeling happy that is lasting (and working on you has lasting effects) creates a lifetime of great moments. Every life is a series of moments. You don't want to be 100 years old with a pile of memories of "trying," you want to be 100 years old with a string of memories of succeeding. It's easier to succeed at relationships with people who are going to be in your life for the long haul. You're a Mama - that isn't going to change. You could move, lose your friends, your job, your - whatever. You won't lose your role. Work on you, work on a fundamental, healthy relationship with your child. It matters more than you think and has long term effects on their life. If they can thrive in your environment you will teach them to thrive in the world.

Income isn't a reason to quit

It doesn't matter if you're on a tight budget, you can connect with your child. If you're rich, I think you really have no excuses. If you're a workaholic you're wasting your time. You can't take it with you, and, no matter how much money you leave behind, your relationships will be cheap, worthless memories you could have developed. Get in the game and do the work. The surprising thing is: kids want to connect with you - so grow out of your coolness and into your goodness. No one cares what your hair looks like today, but we all want to hear how awesome you are.

FUNK
IFIED

FUNK: what matters more than fashion

No matter how many items you buy at the store, have in your possession, or dream about owning - if you're still a rotten bitch on the inside - well, you're still a rotten bitch on the inside. FUNK is a practice. You get a crappy worn out pair of jeans, an old shirt and you start baking cookies until you have fun. Clean the bathroom until you feel like a fricking Goddess. FUNK is feeling "I really can have fun doing this," and "It doesn't matter what I thought I should wear, I feel good in this." FUNK is realizing outside appearances don't always change inside appreciation. Once you master feeling FUNKy in your own skin, the emphasis on outer ownership is put in its proper place. You don't need stuff to be happy - you need Happy to feel happy. I've had some priceless stuff and some shitty junk and how it worked for me (if at all) was completely dependent on my mood. Babies can play in mud, clay, flour, dirt and rocks and they don't care what designer is on their clothes. They FUNK out their fun - you can, too.

Give FUNK its place back in your life so you can relax again.

FUNK is underrated

FUNK is an underrated ability to instantly feel elated. Don't fit in to satisfy the Zombies. Zombies are people trying to look good, trying to be cool, trying to imitate. "Trying" is your clue that they aren't being authentic. Authentic people find interest in almost anything. If it isn't there, they create it. It's natural to have amazement, excitement, laughter and be real. Your FUNK moments come naturally to you, like they do in children. Children who want to sing just start singing. They see something interesting and they gravitate toward it. They don't have time to wonder, "What will the crowd think if I draw this picture?" No, they wouldn't even know how to imagine putting the reaction of others ahead of their interests. Feel like singing? SING! Just let yourself burst out in song at the grocery and, sure, you'll get funny looks. Why? Because you decided to give in to a need to express happiness, joy, and the blissful feeling of being alive. Most people think it's weird. I can't figure out when living became weird, but I don't have time to anyway. I'm busy issuing licenses for FUNKIFICATION all over planet Earth to Mamas who want to feel good. I've been weird to the Zombies for years - big deal.

HERE'S YOUR LICENSE

If you needed a license to FUNK your life, it's on the next page. Just write your name in the blank space and it's official.

Certificate of

FUNKification

This Certifies that

Has successfully completed the training
program requirement for

FUNKification

She has fulfilled all requirements and is a licensed **FUNK** *practitioner*

FIZGIG

YES, it's a real word

A FiZGiG is "A frivolous, giddy woman. A sputtering or hissing firecracker." Frivolous: "unworthy of serious attention." That's how we treat negativity in ourselves, others and material things. Frivolous also means "playful." We're playful in our relationships with ourselves and our children. We don't get these days back. Giddy: "having a reeling, lightheaded sensation, frivolous and lighthearted." "Giddy young girls."

We were expected to be depressed, down, worried, easily knocked off our feet and fall back into a sorrowful hell. We don't want to live there - not anymore. We've found Bliss is real and we are helping each to keep it - no matter what obstacles come up in our lives. There's no sense getting our panties or emotions in a bunch over something that won't matter in a week or a hundred years. FizGiG your butt off. Get giddy, get happy. Being down doesn't help anyone or anything - especially not you or your child. If I could catch you in a down mood the first thing I'd say would be, "Are you done yet?" This isn't mean, it's loving. It means I want you to move on to the next great thought, the next great joy or pleasurable memory-making moment of your life. We all get stuck and pissed off. That's okay! FizGiGs always rock the house eventually, usually in almost no time at all.

The only sputtering and hissing we let pass our lips: laughter, and goofball noises that make our children laugh. Hissing and sputtering noises that can change your mood in an instant are allowed. Broken windows happen. Empty bank accounts happen. Court trouble happens. Dorky men and women who don't know anything about how hard you're working to achieve great dreams happen, too, and they happen way too often. Hiss, sputter and get giddy. I can't wait to hear how fun it was to laugh at your woes while everyone you know sat around bitching. You're teaching your children something valuable: Problems don't define your mood. Your thoughts define your mood and your mood defines how easily you accept your situation and enables you to spot the solutions that are there. Okay, problems can define your mood, but only for a while, and only as long as you allow them to! Dig deep into your fundamentals and pull out a trick to lift you up, so you can see the light coming over the horizon. It won't reach your eyes if you're buried in fear.

Lift your chin, get Fizzy with your thoughts. Whatever happened, happened. Let's fix your mood.

How do you FiZGiG?

FiZGiGing is like being beaten all day while you're carrying a stroller on your shoulder and a baby on your hip. Hateful, glaring, unhelpful people stare at you and want you to fail. You know it, they do it all the time with looks of disgust. You're taking steps down the street of life hoping to find an Inn of Acceptance, a job, money, ideas that help, friendship, humor and just one good night of rest. It feels like you're in a country that hates forward thinking and acting females, but you're in your own hometown, or state. Where do you go now? How do you find inspiration? A FiZGiG digs deep in her soul and remembers...

I'm NOT a single mom!

I'm NOT a single mom!

"I'm a FiZGiG" is far more interesting to hear than, "I'm a single mom."

Saying we're "single moms" has so many negative connotations attached to it. For some crazy reason, it's worse than the plague. It's offensive. I truly believe the only way to change the way other people perceive us is to change ourselves. The negative, whining single moms are creating a legacy they won't want to remember in 30 years (and neither will their children, most likely). To say, "I'm a FiZGiG. I'm not afraid to craft my life, days, moments and memories no matter how bad the deck is stacked," tells the world we're changing the game and playing the hand we've been dealt. Even bigger than a statement - it's a lifestyle with an attitude that we can win this hand. What's at stake? Happiness. Your happiness, my happiness, and the happiness of millions of children.

Get your FiZ on. I need you to change your mind. It's a goofball word for a goofball life that actually matters to a lot of people. None of them are here on my street, but they are everywhere. We are changing the world one crazy ass thought, one crazy ass choice and one conscious act at a time. So go ahead and be different!

Be an amazing soul raising an incredible, amazing child. I am! It doesn't make sense to the people around me who don't get it, but it makes perfect sense to the people who have been there, done that and understand what it's like and do get it. I'm sticking to my F Bomb world and being F-ing fabulous. Because I care about me, and that is all that matters right here, right now.

FLAP DOODLE

REAL WORD? You bet it is

This is where you talk your game.

Flapdoodle is the secret language of a family. The dictionary calls it "nonsense, foolish talk and balderdash."

I'm glad I'm not in school anymore - because Flapdoodle is where it's at in the home. You don't watch TV like you used to when you F Bomb your life. You watch each other. Get in the land of the living and interact with the child in front of you.

See how many times you can make each other scream with laughter. Make up words, code words are great in public. If I don't like someone, or need to get out of a place, my kids know the code. Draw and talk at the same time. Surprise! Intentional word confusion is hilarious! It's as easy as, "Your cakepans are perfectly brewed. Do you want ketchup on your orange juice? Or should I just slice your toothbrush before I ice it for your workhome?" Call them by a new nickname. "Good morning Angel Love Farter! You made the most lovely toots in your sleep last night. The cats were kissing your toes all night long thinking you were a treat from Heaven." Change the order of words to stump and confuse. This is your life! If we rely on TV, video games and paid artists to entertain us we're selling out our Bliss. If you can't put on an ugly dress to make breakfast or dinner occasionally, just for the sake of laughter, then you're losing your creativity to the screen.

There's a lot of great stuff out there, I understand that.

But did you know there's a lot of great stuff in you?

TRANSIT TALK

For some reason we are really well trained to wait for something to happen. We wait for the people on the train to talk first, or the radio to give us something to ponder like the news, a new song or the weather. Forget it. Start now to tune into your life. I don't care if you're living in a shelter or a mansion, it's time to experience your Flapdoodle ability and ROTFLMAO for your family. Families who laugh together take problems in stride. If you can joke, make nonsense and handle day-to-day routines with a little more humor, you'll stop going to bed grateful for the silence and start giggling before you fall asleep. Notice how many moments you can recall at the end of the day that you laughed.

Nobody gets paid to be a serious sourpuss at home - so what's the point?

I can't do it

That's not true, if you give it a chance. Do it with your child so they talk and know nonsense is fun, flavorful, frivolous and flashy. Do it with flare. They'll remember it forever.

FORFEIT

THE TIME TO QUIT

Right now is the time to forfeit (give it up and walk away) everything that was done to, through and against you. The past is over. You can't change it. You can, and must, let it go if you're going to get your happiness back. This isn't coming from someone who has a cushy, easy, or trouble-free life. I've been through "single mom" hell, too. In fact, it lives in boxes in my basement to this day - seriously. However, there is no way I'm going to open them again. All the people who abandoned me, ridiculed, attacked, abused, ignored or didn't give a damn about me or my children live in a couple of boxes.

I put them all together to create an island of **assoholics**. **Assoholics** think they know everything. I don't know everything, and I'm happy to let them go. The only way we get free of the hold the pain of the past has on us is to get free of it! That might look like a really terrible sentence, I know, but read it again.

Forfeit - give it up and walk away. Get here so we can go forward.

QUITTING is the way

There are some things we will never understand: Why he didn't love you. Why "the system" sucks. Why we're "always tired." When we'll get a break. Why we didn't listen. STOP. Some answers aren't figured out, they appear on their own, but only after we let the question go. So for now, walk away and get moving on finding solutions. We aren't going to fix all the problems we are facing in one day (probably). If we spend every day finding possible solutions and moving forward we are way more likely to get our joy and Bliss on track. Quit fighting in any area you know, from experience, that it's not likely you are going to win. Quit everything that is wasting your time. Quit talking with "friends" who are whiners. Quit watching shows about life that are fake and stupid and start living yours. Quit hoping for a man to show up and fix you and fix yourself without a man. No offense Mamas... but you can seriously grow your happiness on your own if you choose. I've never met a baby who waited around for someone to tell them they are wonderful. They know it already. So can you.

HOW do you quit?

People: anyone who isn't cheering you on or engaging in intelligent conversation with you is, I think, a waste of time. Anyone who asks a lot of questions about your life but doesn't have any answers or ideas for solutions is, I think, wasting your story. Anything (shopping, drinking, drugs, TV or social media) that isn't directly contributing to experiencing your life as a wonderful, expressive and beautiful gift is, I think, sucking your energy and stealing opportunities for you to shine. Any thought that says you aren't good enough isn't yours and should be banished. We were born to be joyful. Why not start rediscovering what that looks and feels like? Why would we wait? For what?

FORGIVE

YES, we have to

This can be a tricky one.

I thought forgiveness was about letting someone else off the hook for their behavior.

I thought it meant, "Oh, that's okay, I'll be all right while you keep walking on my soul." It's not that at all. I decided this is what forgiveness means for me, and I hope my definition helps you to move past the feelings of hurt and anger that used to haunt me, too. Forgiveness gives us the sense of beingness we deserve. Forgiveness brings us peace. We extend forgiveness to ourselves, for ourselves. We GIVE FOR BEING whole again. Being whole and complete - nothing missing. If I'm full of hate, I'm missing peace. Resentment takes away my appreciation for myself. Fear robs me of faith in my ability to overcome obstacles. Forgiveness frees you. It may or may not forgive the other person. You don't even have to tell them if you don't want to, but if you don't get anything else about this - get the part where forgiveness frees YOU.

FOR

The dictionary says "for" means "directed or sent to." It's directed or sent to where? To us.

GIVE

Giving is "extending, bestowing." It involves movement. Stay with me on this one, because forgiveness is crucial for healing past wounds. We are "directing and extending..." but what? A gift to ourselves.

NESS

Ness - what is it?

The best, simple term is: Being. "Ness" occurs at the end of most words we use to describe states of being:

- Happiness
- Joyfulness
- Pleasantness
- Playfulness

So we're dealing with: Directing and extending the gift of Beingness. Now that looks ridiculous, doesn't it?

It's not. We want to feel what it's like to BE unburdened by pain, anger, resentment, revenge, hatred and spite.

That way, we free ourselves.

We cannot hold two thoughts at once. If I'm busy hating someone I can't get busy loving myself and my child. Let it go. Being free, feeling happiness, joyfulness and pleasantness we feel alive again. When we are hurting it feels like a little death every minute. We want to get rid of it - forgiveness allows us to release the thoughts that stir up these emotions in ourselves.

FIGHT'ER

As in a WARRIOR

There is a reason to be good at fighting.

Making a loving world for our child and ourselves involves a lot of flamboyant fighting. Consciously fighting old habits and choices every day is work - warrior work. Habits are like individual demons. They secretly plot to thwart our day and our determination to deliver great memories and moments to our children. The art of fighting means focusing on what you want, not what you don't want.

The power of thought

Go to any store and you are sure to find at least one disgruntled, grumpy and unhelpful employee.

This is your imaginary demon, what your invisible demon looks like, on any given day of the year, because negative moods are just disgruntled employees waiting to be recognized. When you feel your Bitch rise to the surface, give her her due. Tell her, "Hello old friend, welcome back to the stage with your unhelpful, time wasting abilities to fool us all into believing you have something to say, when all you do is waste precious moments of life." This will usually cause a quick change to our helpful Diva. Our moods are imitations of how we thought people dealt with difficult situations. Sometimes we watched people, and modeled their behavior. We unwittingly took on the characteristics of Jerk, Asshole and Whiner because that's all we learned. From teachers, parents, coworkers and friends, we picked up their behaviors without examining them very closely.

To change our moods we need to change our players - those internal role models have to be carefully fired if they are the kind of people we avoid in real life. Don't ask your Bitch to do the laundry. Tell her to take a one-way hike and come back when she's healed the chip on her shoulder.

WARRIOR MY ASS

Mamas are well trained by history to feel we are less than wonderful. It isn't easy to keep your chin up when you feel like a loser. Examine the source for a moment. A loser compared to what? What standard are we using to determine our worth? Are we the only women in the world with these problems? Knowing I'm not alone doesn't always make me feel better, but knowing there is an entire generation of children depending on my cheering you on gives me strength I didn't think I had. I don't want to succeed as a Mama just for my children. I want to succeed for yours, too. What am I calling success? If I can create a small world of wonder, ARt, creativity and happiness in my life, home and world then it stands to reason I've changed the world. Wonder, ARt, creativity and happiness are free - and worth fighting for in my life. My corner of the world is all I have to change - one step at a time. That's true for all of us.

FOUNTAIN HEAD

THE DANGEROUS JOY

Over 6 billion people on the planet and YOU are the only fountainhead for your child.

You are the entire world. When our stream of love, confidence, humor, fun, innovation, fierce loyalty and uniqueness runs dry where will they turn? We might look like idiots for trying every possible way to make a terrible situation work, but we're not giving up. We have to be determined to have one successful day... and then ten thousand more. Imagine this: what if every mother who had a rough path ahead gave up? Where would the geniuses come from? Where would the ARtists come from? You play a vital role in the lives of many people you might never meet. Don't give up on you - because this isn't just about you.

"Don't give up. Take a break - but never, never give up on your life." Put this statement where you can see it daily because on terrible, bad days you'll need it. First, to keep going, but also during the times you just have to let the universe unfold on it's own, while you regroup and get your warrior strength up to speed.

We are Fountainheads of and for youth

We are capable of being examples of fierce freedom and fearless dream weaving. If you forget what it means to be in the moment, engage with your child. They are always in the moment without freaking out about past or future. We need this skill so we can focus on creating instead of moaning.

Moaning is for labor and that's over with.

DON'T run dry

We aren't living if we're obsessing about what we don't have.

Try this - if you can tell me your woes can you tell me your opportunities at the same time? Holding two thoughts at the same time is impossible. Stop contradicting your thoughts and wasting precious time. Every day ends, don't lose another minute fretting. We dry up our opportunities if we're bemoaning our lack. It takes five whole minutes for me to think of everything I'd like to own or experience. On any day of the week I lose far more than that to worry if I'm not being the Fountainhead of joy for my children. Did I lose you on this one? It's as though we have compared our lives to what we wanted them to be or become, and then we approach each day as if life has ended. It isn't the end, but we treat it that way. How can we be alive and regret the whole thing at the same time? It's insanity. What is over is the past. What is now is living and what will come has a lot to do with how we are approaching life in real time.

Fountainheads are the sources of life. Children are nothing but original creative fountainheads themselves, all day long. Ask them what they think. Ask them how they play. Get your creative stream overflowing again because you were a kid once, too.

FAITH

IT ISN'T RELIGIOUS

Intelligent scientists don't give up when the experiment fails - they try again. They have faith in success.

They know if they fail they are one step closer to an answer. We all face a series of questions every day. Questions like, "What do I do? How can I get this done? How do I find help? What the hell is happening here?" The difference between how we Mamas and scientists approach life seems to be emotional. We put our worth in with the problem, we question our existence and effectiveness instead of questioning the approach. Every situation is a situation. Period. Medical emergencies aside, sometimes we get caught in the tidal wave of emotion and it paralyzes us. When we stop making situations personal, and let ourselves be wonderful in spite of the situation, we are freed up to be amazed at our own ability to shine.

Have faith in you, your family's destiny, time, change, preparation, courage and healing.

IT'S CONTINUOUS

Why is it we can admit we're really good at some things and yet we think we can't handle today?

Look back over the past few years, or even just your pregnancy. You made it through, didn't you? Maybe you weren't on the cover of People magazine or the front page of your hometown newspaper, but you are the headliner in your own life. There's the problem many of us face. If the world isn't validating our existence or holding our hand or applauding our achievements, we've been trained to believe we don't matter or we aren't successful. I think it's a myth. Your life is a powerful example of personal triumph and will continue to be one. Fifteen minutes of fame might be more than you're ready to handle right now, or it might distract you from the real work of being a happy person and an amazing Mama.

Where do you put your FAITH?

We have to believe in what we can do for ourselves.

Sure, sometimes the world hands us some help. Most of the time we're in this on our own. That stinks.

Does that mean we give up? Having faith in our ability to keep going, fighting our way to peace and happiness, is sometimes all we can do. Write a letter to yourself. Brush your child's hair. Pass time doing things that are neutral, uplifting or calming when you're stressed. If we do things that we think will take away anxiety, but don't, we lose hours and golden opportunities to train ourselves for better lifestyles. We have to have faith that each step, in a new direction, will take us where we want to go. Sometimes faith has to be blind. That's a risk all great world changers know they have to take at least a few times on their path.

We can't be imitators and succeed in life. We drop the madness and accept that we can only be ourselves.

FLOWER

BLINK OF AN EYE

Imagine every moment is a perfect moment - blink - and it's gone. It's perfectly now in your personal hell or it's perfectly now in your personal heaven. How we define it is crucial. It's hard to believe where you are today is going to be one small step in the right direction if you pay attention. It is. We forget life is an unfolding chance to grow, change and be peaceful. We claim our limitations far more easily than we claim our gratitude.

Flowers open silently.

Life unfolds with or without our complaining.

Bliss happens in moments and instances.

Why resist it in this moment?

Why tell ourselves it can't be now when maybe it could be - even with all our "problems"?

FLOW

The strangest thing I used to do was believe I was stuck.

Life is moving, and we fool ourselves by doing the same things over and over every day. We convince ourselves we're stuck, we can't make a difference, be happy or laugh by repeating the same old habits every day. For most people, even taking a walk for ten minutes is crazy, so they don't even consider it. Truth moves mountains because it leads you somewhere. Lies are what we tell ourselves when we don't want to change. Go with the flow, it is a part of existence. Be a Flow-er and watch the load lighten in your life. We're meant to move forward and that means letting go of the lies we tell ourselves about our opportunities. Remember what I said earlier: FREE FREE FREE. Thoughts can be changed free of charge. We have to be willing to trade misery for potential and excuses for muses.

"Mom, why were you always so sad and mean?" probably aren't the words you want to hear in 5 years.

FATHOM

AS ABOVE SO BELOW

There are sleepless nights, blurry days and angry children.

Callous fathers, courts and government agencies come to mind when I think of fathom. Hitting rock bottom, feeling like a loser when people you encounter convince you you're worthless, and the days when nothing goes right can be discouraging as hell. It's easy to stay down if no one gives you hand. Trying to fathom what it all means seems, well, meaningless. It isn't.

Once you have faced the shallowness of people who throw you away, you begin to see the need for being extraordinary. If we don't want to live in a world that discards souls and single mothers like trash, then we have to value ourselves and teach our children to do the same. They will learn to have self love only from us. We have to do it first - or at least let them remind us we have a worthy purpose.

Humble and honorable don't always travel with wealth and title. They often travel alone. So do we.

THINK

Is it true that you can't change?

You may have made some terrible choices in the past, but that doesn't mean you have to make them again. Imagining the ability to be someone different is the first step to becoming the you of your dreams. I suggest walking away from any and all people who treat you as if you can't change.

If they were in my life, I would put them in the basement boxes with all the other **assoholics**.

I wouldn't want them around anymore.

❖

FLING

FAST AND HARD

Fling is what we do with people, ideas, beliefs and systems that aren't helping us live happy lives.

Without even thinking twice about it, into the trash go old love letters that are meaningless, books that remind us of bad times, clothes we wore on dates, jobs or to events that make us cringe when we remember them. Fling every THING that triggers a reaction that's negative in you, and make room for the good. Their sentimental value is making you mental. It's time to give it away to the thrift store or shelter if you don't actually need it, and can afford something new or just do without it for now.

CAUTION: I don't suggest throwing out things that are your child's. Just because an evil grandmother or bitter uncle gave it to them, doesn't mean we have the right to discard it. Ask them if they still want it. If they do - deal with it. It isn't going to bite you unless you let it.

Make it a game

You don't need to cry over the stuff that triggers you. If you aren't sure you can live without it, put it away for a while and come back to it, but get the biggest things, items and triggers out of your sight. It's like circling around the same old neighborhood but wanting to move across the country to a new home. The FREE home is in our thoughts; we have to choose to move. It's simple. It takes a little time, but in the end getting rid of stuff, things and memories is part of getting rid of the past. Forward movement needs a light load.

CATS DON'T HAVE POCKETS

Cats are picky creatures and I like that.

They don't want to be bothered unless it feels good - to them, not you. They don't care if you're enjoying stroking their head, if they're not in the mood they let you know - and fast. Children do this, too. Learn from them both that you don't have to stick around and put up with conversations, people or situations that are bringing you down. Get out of there! Lighten your mental load and move on to a good thing that serves you - it's your time and your happiness.

FOXHOLE

GIRL GETAWAY

"I'm busy." "I can't right now." "Can I call you back?" "Maybe some other time."

No no no no NO!

It's the most powerful word in our vocabulary and we don't use it. Why? Because we feel obligated to show up, even when we don't want to. We're tired, exhausted even. We keep pushing ourselves into new territory, hoping it will offer some magical nugget of hope or change, but it doesn't. We fool ourselves into thinking busy, frantic social lives or scurrying around are productive, when we're just burning energy and not moving any closer to our goal of happiness.

Say, "No, thank you," more. Wait for voice mail - more. Do nothing - more. Doing nothing is a lost ARt.

We think busy = successful, and it isn't true. To be present, available, awake, alert and interacting with our child usually means saying no to people, invitations and events. It's good to avoid things that are a waste of time. How many parties do we need to attend anyway? If it's not an award ceremony for your awesome work on yourself, I think you'll thrive without it and even in spite of it.

Hundreds of hours are spent "hanging out" when we could be changing our life staying in.

POPULARITY IS OVERRATED

I doubt your child cares how many friends you have, what you paid for the clothes they're wearing or where they live. Maybe they do, a little. Even so, our job is to raise complete souls who know worth isn't a price tag or a street address. Children want you to be the most important friend and confidant they have. (Until they're teenagers, and then you might be reduced to mom. If we do this well, that might never happen - because we created a real connection that wasn't superficial). If social life, social media and cocktail parties take priority over baking cookies, drawing together, reading and being together you need a foxhole. A foxhole is where soldiers hide to avoid enemy fire. What enemies? Regret, fights, hangovers, self-delusion and demands that aren't your responsibility. If you thought you could be a social diva and a great Mama, by now you've figured it out - you can't. Those days are gone and hopefully you've gotten over the realization. We need a physical foxhole - where we get away from people and events that reduce our self esteem and an emotional foxhole -where we dodge our inner attacks on our worth. It can be books, journals, music or even a nap.

FULL STOP

STOP means STOP

When the roller coaster of an insane emotion tries to knock you off course, this is the key to freedom.

Refuse to give in to negative thinking. The hardest thing to do when you're angry is to stop. The hardest thing to do when you want to scream is to be silent. Full stop F Bombing is simple and fool proof for preventing major eruptions that we regret - but just because it's simple, doesn't mean it's easy.

PRACTICE

Practice even after you've exploded. Suppose you just let yourself get pulled into a fight with a friend, or had a stupid argument over football or you caught yourself slamming your boss at work with another employee again - the day after you swore you wouldn't waste your time doing it again. Now that you've caught your mistake, replay it in your mind, only this time imagine you being silent. Show your mind how you wish you would have handled it. Giving yourself the answer you want, even after the fact, is how we can train our brains to be ready for the next time. We aren't going to change without practice. We won't change at all if we don't imagine what it looks and feels like to NOT be negative.

SHUTTING UP with your child

The path of raising souls is fraught with difficulties we couldn't predict. Vomit, fevers, broken glass and broken bones - we've never done this before and it can be earth shattering to our systems. It's not surprising we explode, freak out or react in less than angelic ways. Sometimes we are exhausted. One more problem feels like the world is turning inside out, and we can't even catch our breath. Full stops are how to be sure we don't damage our fragile child's self esteem. Thinking through every terrible, nasty and angry reaction, without saying a word, lets you cool off before your lips move you to madness. Stand still, feel the fire, but don't spit flames. You CAN speak with kindness in the face of shocking situations. You CAN keep your hands by your side and not wave them in anger. You CAN blink and remember: this too shall pass. Be grateful you can hold your tongue. Be grateful...be quiet and get a grip on your emotions before you say something cruel, stupid or worthless that leaves a scar on their heart and yours.

FATIGUE

DUH...this is exhausting!

We are learning new ways of thinking, organizing time for a whole family, putting our creativity into every new situation while dealing with paperwork, people and outrageous circumstances that nobody trained us for.

Of course you're exhausted!

ALWAYS ON

We're always on. On the look out for danger: don't touch the stove, don't run out in the street, don't go under the water, don't put a bag on the cat, put on your coat. Where are my keys? Where is my phone? Where's that bill that came last week? There are a million responsibilities we have to take over once we have children, and there isn't a training school for it. Even the books we read on parenting can't predict the next crisis in our daily lives. They can only give us advice after the fact, or so it seems. Fatigue is natural and acceptable. You have cells in your body that help keep you going, but they have to recharge on a daily basis, too.

GET RID OF TIRED

I don't think there's a surefire way to get rid of tired on this path, but there are tricks to preventing it.

Things that require recovery time have to go. Partying is a past time we can't afford and staying up on social media and movies aren't helping you function better in the morning. Make your days creative productions of furious ARt and you'll go to bed tired without needing stimulants from the outside world to make you feel like you participated in life. Your life is your show. Give it the attention and imagination it deserves and watch the hunger for aimless distractions disappear.

❖

FORCE

ISN'T FORCEFUL

Gravity is a force we use every day. It doesn't struggle, though. It just is.

Opening a can takes a certain leveraging force to make it happen. "Nothing happens until something moves" is what Einstein had to say about it, but forcing your child to eat three spoonfuls of peas, because you read somewhere they "should" is a different, and negative, idea. Forcing yourself to get out of bed because you have to is okay. We do it to succeed, to get to work and school on time. Forcing behavior just so that you feel "parentally powerful" often backfires. Force that creates changes in ourselves for the better is great. Forcing your child to go to bed because you want to go out is unfair, selfish and a wasted night - for both of you.

Force means effort. It takes conscious, decisive mental action to stop yelling and start engaging. It takes long, deep breaths to decide what is the best way to handle a situation. It's okay if you don't do things perfectly - we're learning, and we're in this together. That's why we don't give up. Force yourself to ignore the people who expect you to fail. Trust that there are millions of FiZGiGs cheering you on, even if you don't see us or you haven't met us yet. We're here.

FAVORABLE FORCE

Forces in nature that foster growth are quiet, gentle and favorably reliable.

Wind, sun, rain and air have powers that contribute to our health and beautify the planet.

Be the force of love, kindness, understanding and hope. These move emotional mountains in the right direction.

FURY

UH-OH

We all want to lose our cool at times. We all can lose it - but not on someone. Especially not on ourselves. There are plenty of reasons to be furious. We're angry, hurt, tired, mad, hungry, lost, stuck and, sometimes, we feel powerless. Anger is a normal reaction to situations that overwhelm us. Just because it's normal to be furious, doesn't mean we unleash the power of our Furies.

YOUR FURY IS YOUR PROBLEM - deal with her

Children already know you're powerful. You don't have to scream it at them.

They rely on you, and you don't have to remind them how hard you work, worry, wonder and fret. They don't need that. Big people problems are big people problems. Ask for big people help if you can. If you can't find someone to give you sound, doable and intelligent advice, then your creative Muse is due for a solo. You're going to have to pour on all your creative juices and start to work out the problem, and possible solutions, for yourself. In the meantime:

Fury Full Stopping

Get paper and pen in hand and start listing. Get your anger out on paper where you won't say something stupid or do something cruel, demeaning or will regret tomorrow. Bathtub solitary confinement for Mama is an acceptable way to keep you indoors and safe without spending money. Clean the bathroom and grumble under your breath. Tickle your child's toes. Draw on your walls if you have to, (I prefer pencil for these occasional ARtistic events - it washes off easily) but DON'T let your Fury loose on anyone. Even the most deserving asshole doesn't deserve to know they got to you. NO! Keep it to yourself as long as you possibly can and hopefully by the time you COULD explode, you WON'T.

NEVER

NEVER let someone know you're angry if they've been trying to piss you off.

Indifferent silence is one of the things mean people hate the most.

Give it to them - and keep your happiness in tact.

FORGE

A HEAD

Most of life happens in our minds - forge your Bliss.

FORGE #1

The verb.

A. Advance gradually but firmly.

B. To advance with an abrupt increase of speed; shoot ahead.

Both of these are necessary. Some days are slow progress, with little to no sign of getting anywhere. You have to keep going. Happiness is the constant you work on, and situations are where we work on it. Some days we get a jolt of inspiration, and the entire book of secrets to living joyfully is revealed to us - elation is unavoidable, and we get a quantum boost of happiness. Setback days, the ones where we question our sanity, resolve or reasoning, call for remembering our quantum leaps AND our slow progressions. Anyone who contributed to our steps in the right direction, including children, deserves to be pictured on the refrigerator. If you don't have a refrigerator to feature their picture, send them a silent blessing of thanks for reminding you to keep going.

FORGE #2

The noun.

A furnace or heater where metals are heated or wrought.

I see our happiness as what's left after we burn the myth of our imagined weaknesses. When we choose to fire ourselves up for Bliss we end up burning away the impure, unreal and painful aspects of our life, leaving only the authentic, real and exciting reality we were born with. When we do this, we honor our existence, and we honor life itself. These are high aims for one small soul to shoot for, but why aim low? We know what stress, anxiety, pain, worry and fear are like, so it's time to burn off the dross and keep the good stuff. Flinging our bad memories into the forge leaves only the good ones. Fire up the furnace of creativity while you're at it, and watch your boredom go up in smoke - because we are ARting our life. Why not?

We are only aggravating the naysayers, anyway.

FOCUS

ATTENTION HAS A PRICE

What we choose to pay attention to matters.

If I'm thinking about my problems, I'm not giving the answers a chance to come up.

If I spend all day reliving yesterday's mistakes, today is wasted. If I can't get past what my child did in school last week, or last year, I'm not available to help with what's happening today. Remember: focus on what you want, not what you don't want. It's another "simple but not always easy" task - but one that works.

YOU CAN'T SPEAK 2 LANGUAGES

...at the same time. It's confusing.

I don't mean verbal languages, some people are really good at that.

I mean you can't SAY "no, really, I'm not mad" to a child, and be banging dishes and pans all over the place. It's misleading. Get your center, get calm. Sending mixed messages isn't just unfair and confusing for the person on the receiving end, it's a dishonest way to live our lives. We have feelings and we can deal with them. Stuffing them down, or refusing to admit to them, only holds us back from authentic happiness. Focus on the anger, focus on the hurt; feel them. They are emotional experiences that have a message. Learn it, get something out of how you see and deal with the world. Is this how I want to be? Is this my highest ideal of how I can be, or is there something I want to do better? Bringing our truth to the light of consciousness helps us admit the truth and deal with it. Denying what's real is just hiding. Hiding isn't healing. It's just hiding!

CLEAR PATHS

The great thing about dealing with situations as they come up is you get on a roll.

Putting things off causes stress to pile up, and that sucks - for anybody, family or not. The longer we avoid dealing with laundry or dirty dishes they don't go away. They just get, well, smelly. So do situations. They rot, fester and grow heads. They take on a life of shadowy, lurking doom that is prevented when we deal with the facts for what they are. Facts and situations: taking them less personally helps to reveal a clearer path to a solution. Sometimes we make excuses to still take problems personally, DON'T. Do everything you can to see "you" and "the facts of the situation" as separate. Pretending it's someone else's problem can help you work through it. Ask yourself, "How would I tell them to fix this?" How would you advise a friend to deal with this issue? To keep moving toward a higher, more blissful state of being, we have to focus on the choices we have, remain open to new ideas and be willing to try them.

FRE-
QUENCY

MINUTE MINUTES

Tick tock, tick tock. My clock, your clock and every clock on the planet is ticking. Don't think about it.

You just did, but don't think about clocks. No tick tocks, okay? It is nearly impossible to NOT think about something when I just brought it to your attention, isn't it? If you forced your mind to think about blue and pink bunny rabbits, when I said clock, you could do it, if you really wanted to.

ONE MOMENT

A moment is a split second in time. It's magical. It's when anything and everything is happening.

I can't stress enough how everything you experience happens in one split second. That's why we have frequency of thought. If we think about what we want, and ignore what we don't want, we are in a much better position to create positive outcomes and experience happiness. You won't believe it if you aren't doing it - that's why it's magic. Frequently, constantly saying, "I'm going to be happy even if I don't know how," is contradictory. Saying, "I'm happy. I'm happy. I'm so happy I'm **flapdoodling** all day long and nobody cares how funny, funky and free I am but I do, I do!" has an impact on everything.

LESS IS MORE

The less we think about (or talk with) negative people, the more we grow into happy people.

If I take the negative voices out of your life and head what's left? I bet a lot of time for new adventures and creative fun for you and your child. There's also space to heal, think, imagine and design your world. Design doesn't have to be "Plan what your future dream house looks like," though that's a fun exercise, too.

Design means rearranging what you do have until you love it more.

FORE-
THOUGHT

BREAKS

When you've cleared out negativity, the old adage "nature abhors a vacuum" kicks in. You're still here, and you still have the time and space to allow negative thinking back into your life - if you aren't careful. Forethought creates happiness mental fallbacks. The absence of drama and stress will create breaks you didn't have before. You have time on your hands - what are you going to do with it? Think ahead. Plan for these days so when you have an hour, (or maybe just five minutes) you use it to work on something you care about. Make a list of things you want to try, things that fascinate you, or you're curious about. You can break the old habit of letting your mind just wander by focusing your attention on creative thinking, happiness, new ideas and new purposes. This is how we ARt our lives.

ARt

ARting your life is a skill, easily learned and important to practice daily, hourly and every minute.

We ARt because it's natural to express our creative truth. Even though we were born with it, some of us have tried to hide from it, because we're afraid we'll be wrong, or do something that makes us feel stupid. When we start ARting life, we don't freak out about making decisions. Instead, we start feeling grateful for free spaces and time to choose and plan. We remind ourselves, "I have a choice. I can choose what to do here." I suggest creating a list of things you REALLY want to experience in your life. Do you want to have more time for singing, painting, cleaning your bedroom, getting rid of useless items, having your favorite friend and her children over every week? Have you wanted to attend groups, classes, workshops at your local library or meet other cool Mamas? Anything you want to do needs time to do it in.

SACRED TAPE

Taping something to your wall, coffee pot or bathroom mirror helps you to remember it.

True confession: if I'm planning to meet you, anytime after right now, you get taped to my coffee pot. Life flies by some days, and I forget appointments if they're not on the pot. The calendar on the wall isn't even efficient enough, because I forget to look at it sometimes. If it matters, and I don't want to miss it - it goes on the pot. If I tell you you're on my coffee pot it's a compliment.

Tape your "things I want to do - my happiness list" somewhere you will see it every day.

There is no time to kill here, my friend. Don't let time kill your dreams - write them down.

FRAGILITY

SOULS ARE FRAGILE

Things get broken, get over it.

Don't let your Fury shop at Tiffany's. She isn't caring, remember? You and your child are living a legacy of love that has never happened in the entire history of life. Don't let some inanimate object or dinner date screw up your lifelong relationship with your child. It's a trick we've fallen for. All over the world we're told market value is more important than personal or relationship value. It's not true. Look at how people treat you as a "single mother." Your worth isn't determined by that label - unless you fall for that trick, too.

Life is for the living - not something to be shelved.

IRREPLACEABLE FORM

Snowflakes, people, birds, flowers - not one of them are the same.

We've learned to treat rarity with flippant "so what" attitudes. Find a mall with fifty identical purses or pairs of designer jeans and we have to have one of them. What an illusion. We will only have today once, but we treat it like it's replaceable. We polish cars and beat up faces, have diamonds appraised but ignore too many of the chances we have to praise a child we see, meet or know. The fabric of Love is delicate, and needs our attention. We are responsible for forging stronger bonds with the souls we journey with. Attention is free.

Being an F Bombing Mama means we appreciate our child more than the things we buy or own.

REFUSE 2 REFUSE

The "great unknown" is the best part of the gift of raising a soul.

It's full of possibilities and adventures we can't even imagine. Refuse to refuse your child the right to be unique. It's scary to hear their ideas, see how they twist and mangle images and toys, stories and perspectives. In case you haven't noticed: originality is unavoidable. They, like us, are original, one of a kind and this day only people. If the world says they don't fit in, well, good for you. Fitting in is easy in a cattle prodding parade of imitators and naysayers. Being courageously authentic is dangerous - for the fearful. Not for you, not for us.

We might never be famous, rich or perfect... that doesn't mean we refuse our family the joy of being unique.

That would destroy the purpose of being here at all!

FANTASY

PROVE IT

"Prove it."

Has anyone ever said that to you, and you just wanted to punch them in the face? You were just day-dreaming, sharing the details of a nice, simple adventure fantasy and they say, "Prove it." If dreaming good, healthy, happy dreams helps us get through the day - then good for us. Even God's existence is still debated by people today, and I think it's no one's business what we believe or why. Disproved, unproved or improved - studies have shown a healthy inner life is good for all of us.

DREAM ON AND BLESS IT

"Dream on" is often used as a snide way of telling us we can't amount to much of anything in life.

I'm asking you to please, do dream on! It's helping everyone on the planet! Your focused fantasies of a great life will only pull them closer to you, and I think you deserve it. Great inventions come from ideas, and ideas don't get attention if you believe you can't do it or have fun, be happy or enjoy life.

"God Bless it!!!" I once heard a man say his mother always said this. She wouldn't damn a situation, she would ask God to bless it, and make it better. So if you need a good, griping swear phrase I'm bringing it to your attention. It's G Rated to boot.

DON'T RUIN IT

Kids live in a fantasy land and we really don't know what they're destined to become. Telling a child, or anyone, that they're living in "a fantasy land" or they'd better "get real" isn't helping them. You may accidentally destroy the formation of a great idea. Don't ruin their fun (or yours) by thinking your past experiences can predict future greatness - especially your own. If you don't believe it about yourself, how do I know it to be true for you? I believe in your dreams because they are part of who you are.

You can't run away from them.

FANCY

PREFERENCE

It's healthy to know what you like and what you don't like. Preference is a real asset that is often ignored. We give up our right to choose in order to conform to an imaginary popularity club that is boring. Learn from kids: they don't have a problem telling someone "No thanks, I hate orange juice. Do you have any apple?" You're allowed to like what you like. You're allowed to prefer a hot bath over a dinner party. You're allowed to say, "I'm leaving" and walk out of a party that is wasting your time.

FANCY THAT

Imagine a group of older women, dressed in outdated clothing with coiffed hair and faces full of make up. In walks YOU wearing comfortable shoes, a T-shirt and jeans. They tell you, "You look terrible!" and you simply respond with, "Well, fancy that..." and you walk away. You don't have to agree with the masses. You don't have to fit in with every group you run into. You don't even have to fit in with the YOU that was here yesterday. Life is a flow. It's changing all the time. That's part of the beauty of it. You just have to fit in with your healthy, happy, ever-evolving self and fit your child's ever-evolving magnificence in with your time and ARt.

Dress up for fun

Getting dressed up can be exciting and fun. Do it for an event or for the fun of it, but don't let the clothes define you. Threads aren't thoughts. You could be wearing the most expensive dress on the planet, but if you feel depressed, embarrassed, self conscious or worthless the dress won't matter, because you've lost your Bliss. We have to keep the outer attire in perspective. Our inner design will improve over time, because we are weaving moment after moment of self love into our days. Once we love ourselves, it won't matter if we're wearing rags or royal robes - we'll simply feel great to be alive. Clothes are like tools. They may add to our quality of life, but our happiness isn't dependent on them. If your child sees you being happy with what is, while still working on your dreams and goals, they are less likely to believe they can't be happy until they get what isn't.

Happiness is a state of being. It's easy to carry, travels well, but it won't fit on a hanger - it's too big.

Note: We teach children limited thinking, but we don't have to.

FLOURISH

THRIVE

In any moment we can flourish.

Deciding this, accepting this as even possible, changes everything. I can't make you stop crying - but you can. I can't make you believe in yourself, but you can. I can't promise you that you won't blow up at your child again - but you can. You can thrive, but you have to choose it first. Considering all we've been through, it's hard to believe that we might be able to be happy in spite of fear, sorrow, unknowns and losses. I suggest you start by thinking about the sun. It goes through a lot of changes over time. Solar storms cause the Northern Lights, and the magnetic storms generated in the turmoil effect our atmosphere, but it's still the sun. You and I will go through millions of changes, too, but we are still capable of being genuinely peaceful and happy in the midst of any change - no matter how fiery.

SEEDS

Everyone knows that under the right conditions, seeds grow into what they were meant to be. Corn, beans, carrots and flowers all follow the pattern in the DNA blueprint they carry. The critical part: they all need the right conditions to do it. So do we. The difference between us and the seeds we put in the ground is the nutrients, water and light that feed and nourish us, and determine how we ultimately flower, come from the blue prints we create with our thoughts. We can't rewrite our history, but we can rewrite the thoughts that came out of that history. Changing those thoughts, changes our lives - for the good or for the bad. It's up to us. We only need two vital ingredients: willingness & determination. We can want a new life, but we have to be willing to change and be determined to keep changing if we are going to flourish. No one is going to swoop in and just swap it out like it was an old pair of sneakers.

SPACE

We have enough space to grow. Each one of us has room on the planet to think. Breathe. Just breathe and see that you have plenty of room to breathe. You don't have to push anything or anyone aside. You don't have to huddle inside, like you shouldn't be taking up space. Throw your shoulders back. Breathe! You have a right to the room, to the air, to all the freedom you can breathe in. You have enough for what you need to be working on right here, right now. Do that - and make the decision to allow the dead weight of past hurts to disappear, forever. There is enough room for the new you to grow.

One furious, feisty, fierce, fathomable, funky FiZGiGing F-ing minute at a time.

FOLK ETYMOLOGY

FOLK ETYMOLOGY

Changing words, or their meaning, isn't new. Changing what it means to be a single mother - is. The world might be slow to change its view of us - but we can't be. Happiness is too valuable, and our kids need us to go first. If we wait for the world, we're going to miss out on our Bliss. Don't wait.

You can do this. I know you can... I'm doing it right along with you - every minute of every day.

You're allowed to be a **Fancy, festive, flourishing FIZGIG** making dreams out of nothing, **flinging** your woes in the **forge, forfeiting fears** and **flap-doodling** with your **family** - because you matter.

❖

- WORDS TO THROW OUT & REPLACE WITH F WORDS -

F THIS	WITH	OR
WEAK	FASCINATING	FORTIFIED
WENCH	FEME SOLE	FECUND
WOEFUL	FESTIVE	FACILE
WRECK	FEELER	FEARLESS
WHY	FEASIBLE	FATED
WASTED	FANTASTIC	FAMILIAL
WORKAHOLIC	FELLOWSHIP	FAIR
WHINER	FIGHTER	FIXER
WORRY	FAITH	FAVORED
WHY	FORTUNATE	FIRST-RATE
WASTED	FIXITY	FINANCE
WORKAHOLIC	FERVENT	FIERCE
WHINER	FORTUNA	FIZGIG
WORRY	FRUGAL	FLOURISH

F IS FOR FUN - HAVE SOME!!!

FORWARD

I guess some people put that at the beginning of a book.

But this is the beginning of our life. Right here and right now every amazing F-ing event is starting to take place. I know once you close the book, it's easy to get back in the habit of forgetting all you've read and anything I said that inspired you.

You're going to have to take it with you. Tear out the next page and put it on your refrigerator, bathroom mirror or at least write your word of the week or day somewhere you can see it. I've included a couple extra copies for you to give to your friends or any FiZGiGs you meet. We forget so easily that other people are cheering for us. You can email me at fizgiggy@gmail.com. We can't help and encourage each other if we stay behind the curtain of invisible silence. We can't change our lives if we don't give change a chance. This might not sound like something you can believe in, but I believe in you! How can I believe in you if I've never met you? I don't need to see your face to know what you are going through. I don't need to look into your eyes to see the pain you've been through. It's global, and we have to show up for ourselves, our children and most of all each other if we want the world to be better for our children and their future. It's up to us. One person's willingness to allow happiness into their heart changes the entire world. You are that person. I'll keep changing my little spot on the planet, reaching out to women around the world to keep them uplifted and you keep doing it, too. One F-ing thought at a time.

Remember:

I'm not a single mom!

I'm a FiZGiG

Anyone who doubts the coolness of being a FiZGiG doesn't have a clue how cool it is to be one.

FLING FORETHOUGHT FLOWER
FANTASY FLAPDOODLE FOCUS
FORGIVE FLOURISH FREQUENCY
FATHOM FIZGIG FANCY
FIGHTER FORGE
FOXHOLE FUNKIFIED FORFEIT
FUNDAMENTAL FATIGUE FULL
FAITH FRAGILITY FURY STOP
FORCE FAMILY FOUNTAINHEAD

F out of your FUNK

FLING FORETHOUGHT FLOWER
FANTASY FLAPDOODLE FOCUS
FORGIVE FLOURISH FREQUENCY
FATHOM **FIZGIG** FANCY
FIGHTER FORGE
FOXHOLE FUNKIFIED FORFEIT
FUNDAMENTAL FATIGUE FULL
FAITH FRAGILITY FURY STOP
FORCE FAMILY FOUNTAINHEAD

F out of your FUNK

FLING FORETHOUGHT FLOWER
FANTASY FLAPDOODLE FOCUS
FORGIVE FLOURISH FREQUENCY
FATHOM FIZGIG FANCY
FIGHTER FORGE
FOXHOLE FUNKIFIED FORFEIT
FUNDAMENTAL FATIGUE FULL
FAITH FRAGILITY FURY STOP
FORCE FAMILY FOUNTAINHEAD

F out of your FUNK

www.ingramcontent.com/pod-product-compliance
Lightning Source LLC
Chambersburg PA
CBHW040054160426
43192CB00002B/65
9780979493027